Life Lessons

Palewell Press

Life Lessons

Poems by Richard Aronowitz

Life Lessons

First edition 2019 from Palewell Press,
www.palewellpress.co.uk

Printed and bound in the UK

ISBN 978-1-911587-18-7

The cover design is Copyright © 2019 Camilla Reeve
The cover photo is "The evening murmuration of starlings
over Shell Bay, Dorset", taken by Kris Daniel, and we
acknowledge the wonderful image library at
www.shutterstock.com
The photo of Richard Aronowitz is Copyright © 2019
Charlotte Arnold

A CIP catalogue record for this title is available from the
British Library.

I would like to thank the editors of the following publications in which some of these poems have previously appeared:

Anvil New Poets 3; The Bridport Prize Anthology 1999; Envoi; The Guardian; The Interpreter's House; Poems in the Waiting Room (NZ); The London Magazine and *Stand.*

For Henry, my beloved son.

Contents

FOUR SEASONS

Winter

The earth heard about winter again this morning:
it came with the pale fury of hoarfrost and ice on the pond.
Where trees cast shadow at the edge of the wood,
frost whitens the grass like a stain. The winter sun
cannot unlock this iron-willed whiteness.
The winter sun is weak: but tomorrow it will rise
a shade brighter, a degree higher again.

A Pietà in Winter

Grass and earth the shadows of themselves
beneath the yew trees where the snow

has not settled. My dog wanted to eat yew berries
last autumn and I had to pull her sharply away,

fearing the harm they might do her. The berries
are here still: frozen points of colour now

against the blinding white snow and the lesser
whites of the tombs. The gently held body of Christ

drops blood in the snow.

Water Eaton

A skein of birds like a net
thrown upwards at the sky.
It catches you, that sight,
and will not let you go again.
Where do they fly to?

Where are these dark specks
susurrating against the light
drawn to, like iron filings flinging
themselves to the poles –
the magnetism of flight?

Corncrakes

You must not let hand-reared
corncrakes see the stars, the night sky,
until the place and time is right.
Otherwise they will lock on
to the pattern that the constellations
create, at that time and in that place
where they first see them,
and you will not get the young
birds to migrate back to any other
place to breed when they are grown.
That first place where they saw
the stars will be forever the one
for loving and for home.

Grove Dictionary

for Charlotte

Orange blossom, you say?
Life rarely holds such a gentle scent,
yet sometimes my mind goes back
to words I learnt in an orange
grove in Lemonodassos, April 1983:
citrus that shrinks the mouth
into the O of an orange; *sunstroke*
that laid me low for three days;
and *zest* that sustains me
with memories of the blazing fruit,
that sudden revelation of words and light.

Villa Angouletta

I have studied fireflies and seen them belly-laugh
green fire in the night. Their neon language, chemicals
combining to create a monologue of desire in the dark,
sparks in ripples across the olive grove and the undergrowth
combusts with light. It ebbs and flows like a bush fire
picked out of the dark, setting only itself alight.
Below, the Mediterranean sings a different song.
Lights and water; water and light.

After a Summer Wedding, Derbyshire

Dry-stone walls, what have you learned
in your age-old leaning against these hills?
The raindrops on the windows blur their meaning
in the wind as the train rushes on, oblivious
to the beauty we are bearing witness to. The bride
wore white, the groom inhabited a darker suit;
he looked as if something had been ignited behind his eyes:

joy, hope, dread, I do not know. Dry-stone walls
come and go, keeping their metrical time
across this landscape of windswept grass
and huddled sheep. These walls know themselves
down to each last stone. The groom's eyes told me
that it takes a lifetime to understand that it is
the gaps, not the stones, that make a wall.

Whelping

There's still enough wolf in our Springer
spaniel bitch for her to know how to cut

through the umbilicus with her canine teeth,
tear the sac that protects her newborn puppies

and lick away what's left so that they take
their first, miraculous breath, slipping

and mewing out into the world. I take
a breather in the back garden from all

of this new life, wondering how she can know
what to do when she has never given birth before.

The bright sunlight dazzles my eyes
after the darkness of the whelping room.

I blink in the light without knowing a thing
about it before it happens, reflexively.

Mink

I'm full of life to the brim,
the hilt; I'm full-tilt, full-pelt.
I'm as sleek as Lady Muck.

I out-swim water voles, outrun
leverets, outlast elvers. I take eggs
from nests, get minnows by the gills
and pull them out, still gasping.

What catches me, you ask?
A sudden fear when the moon comes up
that unseen hover of wings above a field;
the scentless, snap-toothed steel of a trap.

When a Fox Eats a Rabbit

When a fox eats a rabbit
it eats everything except the entrails.
I mean everything,
                    arse-forwards, headfirst.

On this coruscating morning,
the stomach and guts glisten, still warm,
in the grass. The fox
                    won't be very far away.

The Dream-Lives of Animals

There is something more to them
than meets the eye. They congregate

on street corners, sniff one another,
piss up against walls, that kind of thing.

At night they lie in their rough beds,
trembling and kicking with dreams.

They run to places we can never know,
far from our nightmares of tarmac and stone.

The Shell-Picker

There goes that cry again,
a freewheeling, pulsating *aak-aak-aak-aak*,
and the gull hangs on the air
above the pebble beach, the aerofoils of its wings
moving against the current.
The yellow beak is spotted at its tip with blood.

I dig the blade of my knife
under the lip of the clamshell and see the ripe flesh
like a shy white smile.
It will be a delicious one. The gull looks down
on the pebble beach
and I swear there is jealousy in its eye.

Bonsai

God is in the details
of root and leaf.

I am a giant
against this canopy of trees.

The Commuter

I saw a deer grazing in a field,
its ears and the top of its head just visible
above the ripening ears of corn.

I saw two hares sitting together
and had thought that they were
always solitary creatures.

I saw a fox chasing its long shadow
one early summer's morning
along the edge of a field,

as if it was trying to keep pace
with the train as it sped down the line.
It was soon gone.

I look and look at the beginning
and end of each day from behind
this glass: we are the ones

endlessly in vitrines, while nature
looks back uncomprehending at our display.
I cannot be out there, just yet.

Swift's Hill

It was the hill of my childhood,
where we were taken by my parents
for picnics and long walks in the summertime
up towards the roof of the sky
that lay beyond the woods
that crowned the hill.

I have not been there properly for years,
but I do want to go back to that hill.
What is it that makes me always
drive past and look up at it
from the far side of the valley, but never
turn off down the narrow lane to the valley bottom,
then up to the old quarry of a car park
and make that climb again?

Perhaps it is because I have always hoped
that I would end up there, somehow,
and do not want to go back
until the time is right.

Prelude

After the winding cadence of the road,
we climb the five-bar gate,
printing each stave
with a semiquaver of leaf-mould
and loose grit
from the shattered tarmac.
A pheasant in the field
shrills in alarm
at our approach,
its colours like sunrise
against a canopy
of evening-shaded trees;
skeletons in the closet
of a summer behind us now—
under an unbreakable lock,
turning from a major
to a minor key.

Birthright

The land lies under a patchwork blanket
of fields. All this land is mine:
it is my birthright. All the crows
that scan the fields for seeds,

all the deer that roam along its borders,
all the badgers that dig themselves deep
under my feet are tithed to me.
I am not God, but I am Lord of this estate.

Oil Boom

The sea sucks and spits in slow motion.
Gulls and cormorants disgorged by the ocean
slick the shore, drumming up good trade
in detergents. Soap-box speeches must be made.

JUST HISTORY REPEATING

Bias

All history is subjective,
just as each present is contingent.
What we were and what we are
shifts like sand running over itself:

underneath is permanence,
but on the surface all is movement
and moment and change.
Like cloth cut on the bias,

going against the grain,
or skeins of wool that form tight-bound
worlds that unravel with the pull
of a yarn to be formed

into something else, we unweave
or unwind ourselves to become
something other than we were,
or look at the world with suddenly

fresh eyes, as if it is a miracle
that we are seeing for the first time.
And then the wind drops and the sand
stops still, just for the briefest

of moments, and we realise
that we have not changed at all.
We are what we have always been:
we are just history, repeating.

Winter Moonlight

The cow died in the barn two nights ago
and the geese flew south
when I had thought they were mine.
The heart breaks
and the ice glitters on the pond.

A Heron in the Plague Year

A streak of grey against the grey
of a spring dawn. When it lands
it stalks the bank of the fen ditch
as if it is its feudal landlord,
its bill sharpened on the grinder's wheel
to spear fish out of the water.
Why is it always alone? I never see it
with another one of its heron kind.

A plague has come in from the rats
off the boats on the coast,
some people say. The teeth of pestilence
have eaten my loved ones into the ground,
where they turn with the turning of the soil.
The crosses on our cottage doors
marked the houses with the plague,

and on our short lane no door was left unmarked.
I have cried bitter tears for my son
and wife onto the ground
where the heron walks like a curate.
Sweet spring flowers have sprung up
where they fell. Why did the plague not take me?
The heron knows, but will not say.
The heron is master of all he surveys.

The Sower of Provence

He sowed seeds each day
with the patience
of a stone,
set ten thousand years
on waiting for a god
that perhaps never came.

Trees grew up where he had
struck through, planted
and patted down,
and a forest came
to the place
that each man before
had declared as barren
as a face in Hell.

He walked his woods
each day, this striker-through,
planter and patter-down,
and each day he thanked
a god that came perhaps
to him alone
for the blessing of patience
and green life.

The Cathedral Grimaces

The self-effacing gargoyles,
      ashamed of their own ugliness,
and those sticking their tongues out
      in defiance at the world,
have been sandblasted, carved
      and cajoled back to flawed perfection.

Some day even the question
      of whether all this can really matter
will decay into stony silence,
      to be answered by a blank stare,
beauty and imperfection being
      fleeting as dust devils in the eye of a storm.

Stiff Upper Lip

You have only one chance
to stand up and be counted,
before the peasants lop off your head.

You sit back, hunkered down instead—
afraid of your own voice, leaving
everything that ever mattered unsaid.

The Glass Collector

It is only when you hold up the paper-thin glass funeral jar
that I realise how fine the cage of your fingers is.
You collect glass, perhaps, to defy the history of your family;

to ask: *If glass this fragile can survive, why is it that my grandfather,*
father, sister and mother went to their deaths
after Kristallnacht, and I am still alive? Questions

have tattooed your skin a quizzical cobalt blue to match those eyes.
Were all the glass eyes manufactured under the Nazi regime blue?
Were all the wigs woven blonde? the youngest child in you

keeps asking. How should history answer you? Perhaps by saying
that people endure more than the most delicate antique vase.
Do not allow them to end up in the wrong vitrines of history.

The Manhattan Project

In the old days it was all about the hydrogen bomb:
the melting pot had become the place to plan a meltdown.

The twin towers collapse like rockets in reverse thrust.
It brings to mind other tragedies of an altogether

different kind: those twins Romulus and Remus
who founded a city, standing tall and sleek side by side,

then destroyed each other. New York is the new Rome;
and hatred is as old as the boulders in Central Park.

Confession

Tell it to the blue mountain:
I don't want to hear your confession today.

Tell it to the mighty river:
its currents will make water-sense.

Tell it to the dark forest:
it will hide your secret and never say.

Tell it to the still air:
it will weigh your words with brittle silence.

Tell it to the endless ocean:
it will listen and not make you pay.

Drawing a Perfect Circle

It is deceptively simple; it is not simple
at all. Too many people begin by putting
pencil to paper. They will lose their way,
veer off course, their circle will spiral
inwards or outwards, growing too small

or too large for itself, instead of the fine
tongue from its mouth touching the tip
of its tail in a perfect and endless coiling.
Do not begin with the paper, do not
start with the pencil in your hand. Think;

conjure up a full moon like a burnished
sixpence, let the midsummer sun burn itself
onto the retina of your mind's eye. Now,
putting pencil to paper with your eyes
closed, just draw what you see.

An Art Historian out the Back of a Shopping Centre

Dalí bikes with stamped-on wheels.
Lightweight litter bins that have had
the Picasso kicked out of them until
they resemble heads seen
from many angles at once, just like
his Synthetic Cubist period.
This box of rotten fruit could be
an Arcimboldo face if you squint hard enough.

The Rape of Europa

A million fields between Amsterdam and Berlin,
sewn together by hedgerows and fences
into a limitless skin that covers
the flesh of the earth and the blood spilt on it.

The tip of the plane's wing cuts like a knife
through the oilseed rape below,
that coloniser of those places where armies marched,
tanks rolled and soldiers sang their joyless songs.

Soho, Autumn

Black imprints of leaves like photograms
on the rain-soaked pavements
where the trees hang low
over the railings on the Square.
What are those strange marks
like runes or printer's symbols carved
into the kerbstones along these streets?

Huguenots, Jews, pornographers all came here
looking for something: escape, salvation,
dissolution, a way to make a living.
Who knows what they found
or what found them?
Now the streets are clogged
with rickshaws, bicycle couriers,

tourists, street cleaners
and yet more rain. New arrivals
keep coming and will come again.
They are looking for escape, salvation,
dissolution, life, a living in this maze
of streets. Who knows what they
will find; what will find them?

Downwind

Who'd be downwind from the nuclear
power station, the shitting dog,
the asbestos plant when the wind
blows ill at you?

Who'd be downwind when men talk
and their cruel words rise like a tide
around your ears, when the wind
blows ill at you?

Words

Words are windows and mirrors and walls.
We build a house of meaning with them
and we live in this house undisturbed

for many years until, almost without warning,
there is a new lexicon in which walls are built
to keep people out, mirrors are two-way

and windows give onto only an endless night.
Words become perversions of what they once were:
bad becomes the new good, wrong the new right,

authority is now a synonym for autocracy.
We build ourselves a prison with words
if we do not choose them carefully enough.

LOVE SONGS

South of the Equator

for Charlotte

The position is this, I think,
although I am not sure of the precise
longitude and latitude of my love for you:
you are my North Star, east wind,
south seas and west country.

Now that I am south of the equator
of love, everything is seen
from a different perspective:
your eyes, your hair, your mouth
shine down on me; there's a lighthouse

behind your smile. I'm cast adrift
on the tide, but know that every direction
in which I sail is the only one
when you are its own sweet haven.
You know the signs that tell you

not to swim and not fall in,
those currents that seem gentle
on the surface, but hold you under
their spell and there's nothing you can do?
Well, I am happy to drown in you.

And you, if you're going to fall in love,
                                fall my way.

Sarlat-la-Canéda

for Charlotte

July finds me impoverished by your absence.
The sun beats down on vacant lots
on the outskirts of this town.
Familiar objects name themselves
as morning light plays its fingers
around the whitewashed room
and burnishes the table's surface
where I write these lines.
Breezes drift in and lose their purpose
without your hair to adore.
A clock unwinds above the shelves.

The Red Sea

for Charlotte

The first thing that strikes you
when you come down to the shoreline
        is the utter blueness of it,
like your eyes. The wind weaves
        strands the colour of your hair
from the sand. If you were here
        with me we would leave
two perfect sets of footprints on its blank canvas,
        knowing that the tide would swallow
these hieroglyphs of love.
        As it is, my one-liner can only
tell half the story about us.
        Only with the sunset does the sea
truly, unequivocally learn its name,
        when the redness of the mountains of Jordan
skims the water with reflected glory.
        A first flush of love.

Midnight in Midwinter on Midsummer Common

for Charlotte

The fingers of the treetops
pull down the night sky like a blind.
Moths have eaten stars into its fabric;
it is an old world in which we live.

The town snaps itself out of its revelry
by midnight. The path home from here
will always lead to your street and your house,
wherever you are. This square half-mile of green

has tucked down under the cover
of night and the town is filled with the eye
of the moon. The common is a silver moon-dial
and I am the gnomon chasing my own shadow

around the hours, clutching a trail of mistletoe
plucked from the winter trees made bereft
for you. I am those hands that show you the stars.
I send you a frosted kiss, a gift over the miles.

Old Light

for Charlotte

Even when you close your eyes
you still see light through the semi-
translucent skin of your eyelids
when you look up at the sun.

Even when you close your eyes
at night you still see light dancing
at the back of your eyes, old light
that is an echo of light you have seen.

Even when you close your eyes
you will still see me, your son, your
stars, your moon, your guiding light.
You will see me and know home.

Cusp

for Charlotte

You came into the silence of an unrecorded day,
into the stillness that holds sway
when nature holds its breath.
You did not bring fire or the wheel,
but you changed the world in which I live.

Who are you to disturb nature's peace?
A sunbeam falls perfectly into place.
A salmon leaps against the river's flow.
A songbird sings in an abandoned wood.
Nothing changes; yet something did that day.

August

for Charlotte

The sea shimmers
but it is not phosphorescence:
only reflected light
and the movement of the water's currents.

We are on the same coast
but in different countries: you on the Côte d'Azur
and me on the Costa Blanca.
Funny how one country's language
describes the beach, the other's the sea.
It's all the same to me:
sand and water both move in tides.

What is phosphorescence?
Is it the shimmer that you see on a metal-blue
butterfly's wings; the inside of an oyster's shell?
The aurora borealis?
It is none of these things.

Ships in the night
have seen the South China Sea alight with it.
Like love, it is a chemical reaction:
minute organisms, algae or bioluminescent plankton
in their millions, phosphoresce
a magic carpet of light.

Water is honest: it always tries to be level with you,
but the power of the moon makes the tides;
the wind shapes the waves.

The sea shimmers
but it is not phosphorescence:
only reflected light
and the movement of the water's currents.

Night Song

This much I know: when we ask questions
we are often answering another need
than understanding. I do not wish to know.
I want to hold you, to find the sleep that you exhale.

Sound lags behind the silence that laps at you constantly.
The moon rises and falls, waxes and wanes
like the tides of sleep. The crescents of your fingernails grow.
The ancient constellations of your eyes grow older.

Your lips might spill the breath of a prayer
that flutters like a butterfly, settling. I wait to catch it,
to net its sleep-encrusted meaning. Where are you,
who are you when you're dreaming?

Pastoral

And up to the burnished roof
of the sky, and beyond the sky
only the moon and the stars.

"And what is beyond the stars?"
you ask, aged four, as we climb
to the top of the hill in the half-light.

"Love," is all I can think to answer you.

Dark Twin

Life has pitched us against each other,
one for evil, one for good. Somehow
I always knew it would.
Born in the womb, you died at birth,

you destined for the ground, me destined for the earth.
Dark twin, your constellation is the cluster
of soil. Dark star, mercilessly loyal
in your trajectory that mirrors

the rise and fall of my days. A story
of a shadow and its familiar; stray
choices that could have been taken
playing off the choices I have made.

Mountains mirrored in a lake,
your fjord-calm reflections
of the directions that I choose; the codes
by which I live, codes that you attempt to break.

Steering a course by someone else's star
grounds you; wrecks you on the rocks
of having only got so far by yourself.
Dark twin, your consolation is the pole

star of my inheritance. Your anchor
drags like a lode stone, but is the magnetic north
against which I navigate. My compass
is the radius of my conscience;

you trespass on the longitudes and latitudes
of my life, but cannot deflect my course. Dark twin,
I'm tuned to your whispered frequencies,
but you're gone now. All I get is static and radio silence.

Poem for a Boy

He was just a kid: a white baby goat
that we nicknamed the "escape goat".
When you were small, he got through

the fence of the garden of the holiday house
where we were staying and made
a break for freedom down the road.

He realized soon enough that freedom
was not all it was cracked up to be,
and missed his mother and bleated

on the road until we rescued him.
Young boys when they grow to be men
will remember such epiphanies as this,

should they find themselves alone
on a quiet country road, their mothers
light years out of earshot.

The Holy Bible

If I had the words, I would tell you
how the last of the snow had not yet melted
when the cherry blossom came, the simple trees
suddenly incandescent with life,
light as air but freighted with the weight
of what would come.

If I had the words, I would tell you
how, later, the cherry blossom caught the last
of the sunlight, unmoored itself on the dying
breeze and sailed away, settling
in the hedges around our garden
like confetti after a spring wedding.

If I had the words, I would tell you
how our love will not be scattered to the winds
when you are gone – but I am
dumbstruck by your silence.
You are drifting beyond reach now,
one hand in mine, the other on the holy Bible.

A Scattering of Light

Those stars that you see,
picking holes in the fabric of the dark,
went out light years ago.

These hands that hold you
in this night's stillness held the hands
of my mother as she lay dying,

blood clots blooming under her skin.
Her ashes that I scattered – irreducible carbon
and immolated bone – were the same stuff

as diamonds and she lasts forever
through you. Where were you, my son,
my darling, when she was fading

to nothing, when she was gone?
The star-shine and moonbeams
thread themselves through the water here,

a scattering of light.

Morning Prayer

Let us not say
what needs to be said.
Let us prevaricate,
delay, desist.
Let us not wake the dead.

Let us not do
what needs to be done.
Let us down tools
of speech, clam up, keep shtum.
Let us not come undone.

Surfacing

The cracked Formica almost drove you mad,
the way it caught the sleeves of your pure new
lamb's wool sweater. The film of dust

that coated every surface, every plane
of every object – "Too near the coal mine,"
you used to say – colonised your household

habitat the more you dusted it. The cake
of make-up that you lavished on your cheeks,
your eyes, your lips, was eaten by each day

and spat out on the pure new whiteness
of your pillowcases and your single sheets at night.
You always found the arrangement of the gravel

on the pathway up to your front gate somehow
asymmetrical. Your colleagues' talk swam
on the surface of things, while you dreamt

of dipping below the noose of scum that chokes
the weir to see what lay beneath: it was that
or escaping to the Caribbean to learn to swim.

It has been three days now that the police
have searched your favourite stretch of river.
They have found nothing, which on the surface

is good: yet your passport is still lying
in your bedside drawer. I might have to wait
until the spring rains swell the river, the divers said.

The Lost Art of Knife-Sharpening

That image of your father standing
by the kitchen range never leaves you,
how he stooped to inspect the Sunday roast,
and then, with the blade glinting,

dismembered wing from body,
dissected leg from undercarriage.
He straightened up again to sharpen
the carving knife on the whetstone

that he held sceptre-like in his left hand.
"You have to caress the blade until it sings,"
he said. "What you do with it after that
is up to you." But you were young

and did not understand the skill it took to hone
the blade to an edge as sharp as your father's wit,
as keen as his intelligence. Yours were blunter,
then. Your father gave you many things:

his love of language, his distaste for authority,
an English reticence, standing back when others
push themselves forward – but a talent
for sharpening knives was not one of them.

Putting up a Music Stand

for Michael Donaghy

It's been years since I have thought
about one of these: how you have
to unfold the stand section by section,

rotate or turn the elements pin by pin,
make parallels into rhomboids and rectangles
until it begins to make sense, to find

its own coherence. The whole is no more
than the sum of its parts, yet so much
more. It's how music itself takes shape:

from abstract points on lines to something
absolute, made real and beautiful
through our manipulation of the parts.

New York, Fourth of July

The yellow cabs in your black neighborhood
streak by like mustard on a hot dog,
full of the juice of gasoline. You climb the stairs
and the thirty-fifth floor of your
high-rise with its elevator laid low is,
for one night only, the best place to be.
The sky's gunpowder-plotted astrological chart
has your stars in the ascendant, going off
with paparazzi flashes of promise.
The Chrysler building, its lights like spilt milk,
blasts upwards over Midtown, failing to launch;
a rocket with its touch-paper keystone
held for a moment, then another and another,
by the car lights along 43rd and Lex.

The cab driver's name is Monplaisir,
and you tip him five bucks for the pleasure
it gives you. A quarter to nine on the Fourth of July:
from Flushing Meadows to Bryant Park, from the East
to the Hudson rivers, fireworks flash against the canvas
of the dark, abstract expressions of something
just beyond your grasp. Well, reach up,
catch them as they fall. The crowd's roar drums
tinnitus in your ears. Lights fountain down,
the sieved rays of multi-coloured suns. Let them come.
Walk the sidewalks, be among people,
smell the cordite, sift the night for the one
who was sucked through the eye of a needle,
a hole in the sky, from your life. The light of your life.

The Day I Almost Went to a New York Yankees Baseball Game

for Charlotte

Sometimes life's like that.
The ballpark was full, even the bleachers,
so we ate Sweet Italian hot dogs
outside the Yankee Stadium, hearing
the crowd and the jingles
and the fanfares and the commentators
with their fill-ins covering all the usual bases.

We headed down to Brooklyn and took a D train
on to Coney Island, baby, the place that Lou Reed
sang about and which has always had
something of his Walk on the Wild Side
about it for me. We took a walk along the Boardwalk
and rode the nineteen-twenty-seven wooden roller
coaster, as rickety as a shack but twice as fast.
Up towards Brighton Beach and the talk's
all Russian and the food's all blinis and the drink's
all ice-cold ice buckets with their pearlescent sides
holding bottles of Stolichnaya like white flags
in bars called Tatiana's & Natasha's.

The freak show's one man,
two women and an albino six-foot python
who conjugate and recombine
in many Amazing and Novel ways.
There's fire-eating, sword-swallowing
and arm-piercing, but even the man's
beardless (I so want to see a bearded woman).

Out into the saturated air again, down
to the water's edge. All life is here and crabs
and jellyfish lie prone to the gulls
that snap back to earth again and again
as if on elastic. The sun falls into the Atlantic
like a giant Ferris Wheel at precisely
six forty-five and the music and dancing
begin again at Tatiana's and Natasha's.
The gulls wheel and turn in a mazurka
to the sheer pleasure of flight. But
even they cannot leave this place.
All life is here except you.

End Station

Parallel lines meet at infinity,
but in the case of these rails they stop
a long way short of that: at the buffers
and the traveller's buffet, at
the men's toilets with their
I LIKE MEN LIKE U and the women's
with almost the reverse
of this graffito paradigm.

Isn't this where the idea
of the soul comes in, the whole
being worth more than the sum of its parts?
Around these parts, this hole, the soul
is hard to find and the devil has crept
into every corner, scattering scraps of litter
that stain the tarmac like confetti
at a Town Hall wedding.

What do we do with places like these?
We live in them and maybe fall in love
in them, we hate in them and hate them
because they are going nowhere.
We bypass them and go up-line
to other towns that look the same:
identical shops, identical Braille of chewing gum
on the pavements, similar birth-, death-
and crime-rates, similar loves and similar hates.

Parallel lines meet at infinity,
but in the case of these rails they stop
a long way short of that: at the buffers
and the traveller's buffet, at
the men's toilets with THE TOWN
THAT NEVER HAPPEND
and the women's with almost the reverse
of this graffito paradigm.

Richard Aronowitz (b. Cuckfield, Sussex in 1970) has published three novels: *Five Amber Beads* (2006), *It's Just the Beating of my Heart* (2010) and *An American Decade* (2017) and they have been reviewed in *The Financial Times*, *The Guardian*, *The Independent*, *The Independent on Sunday*, *The Jewish Chronicle*, *The Spectator*, and *The Wall Street Journal*.

Richard's poems have been shortlisted for the Bridport Prize and the Troubadour International Poetry Prize and eleven were anthologised in *Anvil New Poets 3* (2001). His poems have also been published in *The Guardian* and *The Independent* newspapers.

Palewell Press is an independent publisher handling poetry, fiction and non-fiction with a focus on books that foster Justice, Equality and Sustainability. The Editor can be reached on enquiries@palewellpress.co.uk